EVERYDAY
STRESS RELIEF

ESSENTIAL TECHNIQUES TO BOOST
EMOTIONAL RESILIENCY AND
IMPROVE YOUR HEALTH

RUTH C. WHITE PhD

**ROCKRIDGE
PRESS**

D1115333

Copyright © 2020 by Rockridge Press, Emeryville, California

No part of this publication may be reproduced, stored in a retrieval system, or transmitted in any form or by any means, electronic, mechanical, photocopying, recording, scanning, or otherwise, except as permitted under Sections 107 or 108 of the 1976 United States Copyright Act, without the prior written permission of the Publisher. Requests to the Publisher for permission should be addressed to the Permissions Department, Rockridge Press, 6005 Shellmound Street, Suite 175, Emeryville, CA 94608.

Limit of Liability/Disclaimer of Warranty: The Publisher and the author make no representations or warranties with respect to the accuracy or completeness of the contents of this work and specifically disclaim all warranties, including without limitation warranties of fitness for a particular purpose. No warranty may be created or extended by sales or promotional materials. The advice and strategies contained herein may not be suitable for every situation. This work is sold with the understanding that the Publisher is not engaged in rendering medical, legal, or other professional advice or services. If professional assistance is required, the services of a competent professional person should be sought. Neither the Publisher nor the author shall be liable for damages arising here-from. The fact that an individual, organization, or website is referred to in this work as a citation and/or potential source of further information does not mean that the author or the Publisher endorses the information the individual, organization, or website may provide or recommendations they/it may make. Further, readers should be aware that websites listed in this work may have changed or disappeared between when this work was written and when it is read.

For general information on our other products and services or to obtain technical support, please contact our Customer Care Department within the United States at (866) 744-2665, or outside the United States at (510) 253-0500.

Rockridge Press publishes its books in a variety of electronic and print formats. Some content that appears in print may not be available in electronic books, and vice versa.

TRADEMARKS: Rockridge Press and the Rockridge Press logo are trademarks or registered trademarks of Callisto Media Inc. and/or its affiliates, in the United States and other countries, and may not be used without written permission. All other trademarks are the property of their respective owners. Rockridge Press is not associated with any product or vendor mentioned in this book.

Interior and Cover Designer: Rachel Haeseker
Art Producer: Hannah Dickerson
Editor: Carolyn Abate
Production Manager: Riley Hoffman
Production Editor: Sigi Nacson

Illustrations © 2020 Pavel Fuksa; Shutterstock/Alex Blogoodf, cover and pp. VI, XI, XII, 32, 50, 70, 77, 88, 104, 117, 123, 126, 132.

Author photo courtesy of Mel Ponder Photography

ISBN: Print 978-1-64611-576-1 | eBook 978-1-64611-577-8

R0

EVERYDAY STRESS RELIEF

This book is dedicated to anyone who
ever wanted to exit the rat race—
if even for a minute—to take a
long, slow walk in the sunshine.

Contents

· · · · · · · · · · · · · · · · · · · ·

Introduction

Stress is something we all experience, and yet we all cope with it in different ways. What triggers the stress response in one person may not impact another. Learning healthy ways to deal with whatever stresses *you* will reduce the negative impact of it on your mind and body.

My own experience with stress is what inspired me to write my first book on stress management, *The Stress Management Workbook: De-stress in 10 Minutes or Less*. I live with bipolar disorder, and my first two books focused on how to prevent and manage the episodes of mania and depression that characterize this illness. These books were written as a result of a hospitalization that led to an exploration of what triggered my episodes. I was inspired and motivated to keep my career by searching for holistic approaches that would avoid the negative side effects—such as impaired brain function and risk to liver and kidney function—that are common features of most psychotropic medications.

I deployed my academic research skills to learn all I could. I soon realized that I couldn't change my predisposition to this chronic and severe mental illness, but I could reduce my risk of symptoms. And at the core of that was reducing the stress in my life, managing the stress I could not eliminate, and building emotional resilience.

I won't lie; at first it was a struggle. As a single mother of one child, with a full-time job, my daily life included juggling the demands of work and the obligations of single motherhood (with an out-of-state co-parent). All of this while trying to squeeze in self-care, such as a basic beauty regimen, an exercise routine, a passion for travel, and my love of the great outdoors expressed through hiking and kayaking.

What I quickly learned was that if I did not control my stress, I would most likely end up on disability due to the frequency and severity of my symptoms. So I learned to prioritize what was important and learned to take life in stride. Since that time, I have found that the primary keys to my success in maintaining my good health include:

- proper sleep hygiene
- good hygiene
- healthy nutrition
- regular exercise
- practicing mindfulness
- the company of people whom I love and who love me back

These actions built my emotional resilience so that when I experienced emotional distress, my mind and body were prepared to engage and resolve whatever the problem was—without risking my mental or physical health. I was offered an opportunity to serve as a mental health consultant to a Fortune 100 company and asked to develop a workshop on emotional resilience. The materials I prepared became the foundation for a consultancy in stress management and compassion fatigue. They also informed my first book on stress management and served as the foundation for this one.

This book outlines a wide range of common stressors and tailored responses. It focuses on four key strategies: writing, movement, mindfulness, and reframing, or thinking. You will learn how to identify your stressors and triggers, and will be presented with concrete actions that respond to the kinds of everyday experiences that may be a source of tension in your life. I hope you will use this book to develop a set of personalized strategies that work for your unique stressors and your unique responses, so that you can have a healthier and happier life both at work and at home.

As you progress through the book, you may wonder if the strategies are working. Most of us are aware of the ways we respond to stress and know when we are feeling stressed out. We are familiar with our cues, from shortness of breath to excess sweating to a piercing headache. We also know what calm feels like—clarity of thought and focus, solid sleep. After practicing the strategies outlined in chapters 2 through 6, you may not end up with the demeanor of a Buddhist monk, but you will feel relief from your most distressing stress symptoms.

Chapter 1

Cultivating a Healthy Relationship with Stress

We all experience stress, and it isn't all bad. A certain amount of stress is a good thing! In this chapter, we will discuss why stress is important and how best to manage it so it can become a positive influence on our life, rather than something that drains us, breaks us down, and causes sickness or illness.

Why It Matters

Stress that we experience in a moment when we need to perform at a high level—such as an important speech or athletic performance—is good for us. It keeps our brains sharp and alert, and our bodies ready for a challenge. However, when we experience long-term stress, or we feel overwhelmed by the stress of a demanding situation, our mind and body react in ways that are counterproductive. Often our physical symptoms of stress can leave us feeling ill. It's vital to learn that we can't always control the sources of our stress—such as a demanding work schedule or a long commute—but we can control our responses to that stress.

I can't promise you that this book will turn you into a Zen master who calmly deep-breathes their way through all the stresses of life. But you will have the opportunity to identify what your unique stressors are and develop stress management strategies that work for *you*. Here are some of the benefits of a healthy relationship with stress:

Teaches Emotional Resiliency

To cultivate a healthy relationship with stress, it's important to build emotional resilience. This is the ability to actively and creatively adapt to stressful situations and crises. In other words, it's how you bounce back from the difficult moments. Building emotional resilience keeps your body and mind prepared for the ups and downs in life so that when they inevitably come, your reactions won't create a negative impact on your life. To some degree, emotional resilience is something people are born with. Some people tend to be more sensitive to stressors than others. Aside from our natural tendency to seek out peace and calm during the storms of life, other characteristics can impact how we react to stress. These include age, gender, and exposure to childhood trauma. But regardless of your hard-wiring, the good news is that emotional resilience is also something that can be developed.

The three dimensions of emotional resilience include the following:

Physical elements, such as physical fitness, health, and energy.

Mental or psychological elements, such as self-regulation, self-esteem, emotional awareness, self-confidence, internal locus of control, problem-solving skills, flexible thinking, attention, and focus.

Social elements are the facets of the interpersonal relationships we have in our lives, such as a supportive network of friends, family, and colleagues, and our levels of likability, cooperation, group conformity, and communication.

Promotes Brain Growth

The whole idea behind a growth mindset is that the brain can grow through the practice of certain behaviors that increase our neural connections. Research has shown that building resilience through good nutrition and sleep habits can increase our neural networks and thus brain performance.

Improves Physical Health

A healthy relationship with stress also improves physical health. Research shows that stress is one of the top reasons patients visit their primary care physician. One of the ways stress negatively impacts health is through the release of cortisol. This is useful in the short term, but a constant stream of cortisol can cause long-term chronic inflammation, which can damage blood vessels, make joints painful, and increase the risk of cardiovascular disease and insulin resistance. Other physical responses to stress can include asthma attacks, hypertension, and gastrointestinal disorders such as heartburn, diarrhea, ulcers, acid reflux, constipation, and irritable bowel syndrome. Some people also experience tension headaches or muscle pain, or grind their teeth. Prolonged stress without intervention can result in significant impairments to health. This is why learning to manage your stress is a powerful predictor of health and well-being. If you are reading this book, you are already on your way to being healthier and happier.

Neuroplasticity

....

Neuroplasticity is the ability of the central nervous system of the brain to learn and adapt throughout its life span. The term "neuro" is short for "neurons." These are the nerve cells that are the foundation of the brain and our nervous system. The term "plasticity" refers to the adaptability of the brain. Also known as brain plasticity or neuro-elasticity, it's the changes in brain pathways and synapses that are the result of interactions between neural processes.

Prior to the 1960s, it was believed that the brain stopped developing after infancy and early child-hood. Current brain research now shows that new experiences and knowledge can cause the brain to alter existing neural pathways and develop new ones. In normal development, the brain changes to maximize performance as we learn and grow, which is *structural plasticity*. This is best defined as changes to the physical structure of the brain, usually a result of learning. This tends to vary by age. So in infancy and early childhood, there is rapid growth of neurons and the connections between them known as synapses. However, as we grow, we lose synapses because those that are used frequently develop stronger connections and those we rarely use tend to die off. This is a process known as synaptic pruning. In many neurodegenerative diseases, there is a significant depletion of specific types of synapses in key areas of the brain.

In the case of injury, neuroplasticity allows the brain to reestablish normal behavior. For example, children who have experienced brain surgery to reduce seizures experience significant recovery of language and motor functions, and after a stroke, motor function can be restored. These are two examples of functional plasticity, which is the ability of the brain to move a function from a damaged area to an undamaged area.

How This Book Can Help

Like nearly everyone on the planet, you experience stress in your life, from a demanding job that has you working long hours, to a long commute, to raising an unruly teen, to supporting an elderly parent. After all, even finding time to run errands and take care of yourself when your dry cleaner and dentist are only open during weekday hours can prove to be challenging.

Even if you are one of the lucky people who can work from anywhere and at any time, you may still find work challenging. When your office is a laptop and your meeting room is virtual, it's easy to blur boundaries about when to work and when to rest. And if you live in the United States, where there are no legal requirements to provide vacation and no government-mandated maternity leave (except in a handful of states), the limited time you have away from work can leave you chronically tired and put you at elevated risk for stress-related medical conditions. These conditions may include insomnia, migraine headaches, hypertension, anxiety, depression, weight gain, and gastrointestinal distress.

Even if stress has not yet sent you seeking help from a medical professional, you may find yourself feeling more irritable and short-tempered. So . . . what can this book do for you?

First, it is important to note that a healthy relationship with stress is possible. It doesn't have to be the bane of your existence or keep you up at night and make you dread the mornings. In this book we will explore the body-mind connection and focus on your emotional, psychological, and physical responses to stress. You will learn new strategies to manage and mitigate how stress impacts your overall health and happiness.

There will be a discussion of the most common forms of stress that people experience and a collection of research-backed strategies for relieving stress that build emotional resiliency, improve brain health, and stop the negative health effects of stress on the body. The key to this book is the solutions— exercises based on psychology, mindfulness, and movement. These types of exercises will help you build a toolbox of strategies for reducing the impact of stress in your life, boosting brain health, improving physical health, and building emotional resiliency.

Research-Backed Exercises

Changing the way you think is one way to manage stress, build emotional resiliency, and boost brain growth and physical health. For example, the stress of worrying whether your child will succeed 15 years from now, or whether you will fail at that sales pitch in your next meeting, is a result of how you think. Reshaping your thought process will reduce how much stress you have. If you shift from thinking that you are going to fail to telling yourself you are going to succeed, you're much more likely to feel less stressed. As the American philosopher and first educator to offer a course in psychology in the United States, William James, once said, "The greatest weapon against stress is our ability to choose one thought over the other."

Perhaps you are afraid of public speaking. You're convinced you'll forget key points or that no one will care what you have to say. You spend so much time thinking about all the ways you will fail that your hands get sweaty, your heart races, and you can't even think about what you have to say. Instead, what if you focus on the fact that the audience really wants you to succeed and is rooting for you, that you're an expert in what you do and can step out onto the stage with confidence instead of being afraid?

You can literally change your life by changing the way that you think. There are several psychologically based techniques that you can make use of to manage the stressors of your life. These include:

Visualizing the activity. Conducting a step-by-step mental walk-through, or visualization, of an activity or event may prove beneficial. A number of professional athletes use visualization to perform at their best. For example, USA gymnast Simone Biles has talked about working with a sports psychologist to perfect her performance and feel confident enough to execute very complex athletic feats.

Visualizing calm. Visualizing a calm place or feeling can slow your heart rate and breathing, and lower the amount of cortisol and adrenaline in your bloodstream, key steps to reducing symptoms of stress. It can be anything you consider calming—that feeling when you've just had a massage, or are sitting on your favorite beach doing nothing, or are experiencing the silence of a forest during a walk.

Repeating mantras or affirmations. Repeating phrases or mantras is known to help build emotional resiliency by shaping the way you think about yourself. For example, if you wake up every morning and see stickies on your bathroom mirror that express your capabilities, you begin to build emotional resiliency by thinking positively about yourself and what you can do. This exercise will cause any doubtful feelings about your abilities to be pushed out of your mindset and be replaced by feelings of success.

Mindfulness-Based Exercises

These days it is hard to avoid the topic of mindfulness as we get more conscious of how constant distractions can make us feel stressed. For example, while writing this book I had to avoid my social media accounts. I also scheduled my email check-ins so that I didn't find myself doing everything but what I needed to do, which was write. I turned on the Do Not Disturb feature on my phone so it wouldn't ping me every time someone was trying to connect. Mindfulness keeps us fully in the present moment, focused on one thing at a time, allowing us to deeply experience our lives. It also allows us to be more productive and efficient. Even with all of those benefits, a lot of people find it difficult to turn off their brain and focus on the moment. Sharon Salzberg, a leading teacher of Buddhist meditation practice and bestselling author, sums up the practice with a good reminder that "mindfulness isn't difficult, we just need to remember to do it."

Sometimes mindfulness is as simple as taking a long, deep breath with your eyes closed. Doing that will slow down your breathing, bring more oxygen into your bloodstream, and boost brain growth by increasing cognition and focus. Taking a deep breath also helps build emotional resiliency by allowing you to be more in control of your emotional response to stressful situations, such as a crying toddler, endless emails, or sad news about a loved one. If you apply mindfulness to your eating by actually taking a lunch break and focusing on the tastes and textures of your food, you enjoy your food more and improve digestion, and reduce gastrointestinal symptoms of stress, such as indigestion, acid reflux, constipation, etc.

Movement-Based Exercises

Our bodies were meant to move. But the 21st century lifestyle is getting more sedentary. We order groceries and meals with apps or grab an Uber instead of taking a walk. We spend a lot of time in front of screens, from laptops, to phones, to TVs. According to a 2018 report from the Centers for Disease Control and Prevention (CDC), between 2007 and 2016, obesity rates increased from 34 percent to 40 percent, and severe obesity went from 6 percent to 9 percent. According to the World Health Organization, at least one in three adults is overweight. The organization sees a direct correlation between weight gain and an increase in heart disease, stroke, diabetes, some cancers, and musculoskeletal disorders such as osteoarthritis.

Adding more movement to our lives is one way to reduce our risk of disease, plus simple activities such as walking increase mental clarity and performance. A lifestyle that includes regular workouts—yoga class, running, hiking, and so on—builds emotional resilience by keeping your body and brain fit to handle emotional or psychological distress. Mastering physical activities can also promote brain growth, in addition to the obvious boosts to our physical health. But even if you haven't developed a consistent practice of movement, you can use physical activity in the moment for a healthier response to stress. Some of the stress-busting activities that we'll discuss in this book include yoga, stretching your neck and shoulders, and taking a quick walk around the block to burn off excess energy. Fresh air and sunlight have the added bonus of boosting mental health.

What Is Stress?

Stress is an evolutionary response to changes in your environment. That change can be physical, emotional, psychological, or behavioral. It is a state of mental or emotional strain or tension resulting from adverse or very demanding circumstances. It's that feeling you get that there is too much emotional or psychological pressure. Stress in small doses and at the right times helps you perform demanding tasks and appropriately respond to risk and danger. It can be a healthy response to life's challenges. However, prolonged stress is not good for you.

The hormones released during a stressful experience, adrenaline and cortisol, can be detrimental to the mind and body if constantly released over a long period of time. It is also important to know that what's considered stressful for one person may not be for another. We are hardwired and socialized to respond to stress in certain ways.

Let's talk about adrenaline (epinephrine) first. This hormone speeds up your breathing and heart rate, which increases the flow of blood to our muscles and our brains. It also triggers the body to metabolize sugar for us to use as fuel. This is all to help us respond quickly to whatever is happening. Cortisol is the other key stress hormone that gets released during a stressful experience. In the short term the hormone reduces inflammation. However, chronic levels of cortisol can increase sugar, triglyceride, and cholesterol levels in the bloodstream, as well as blood pressure.

Other impacts of high cortisol levels include the buildup of plaque deposits. All of this can lead to damaged blood vessels, which can lead to cardiovascular disease, or insulin resistance, which may cause diabetes. Painful joint diseases, such as arthritis, are another potential result of chronic stress. Because of these impacts of stress hormones on the body, prolonged exposure to stress can not only exacerbate illnesses but also cause them.

There are three key ways our bodies respond to stress:

Fight. We stand our ground and defend ourselves, whether emotionally, psychologically, or physically.

Flight. We run away, and that may mean metaphorically by psychologically avoiding the source of the stress or actually physically leaving the room.

Freeze. We find that our brains have "shut down" and we are unable to "think straight" and sometimes find ourselves feeling as if we are physically rooted in one place.

Our physical responses to stress are wide-ranging. They can be minor, such as increased sweating, quickened breathing, heartburn, head-ache, acid reflux, grinding teeth, or reduced sex drive. Behavioral responses include smoking, drinking, eating too much or too little, and emo-tional and psychological responses such as anxiety, depression, irritability, and anger.

A Brief History of Stress Management

The word "stress" is derived from the Latin verb *stringo*, which means "to draw tight." Seems appropriate given the bodily tension that results from stress. The pioneering endocrinologist and stress theorist Hans Selye is said to have borrowed the word "stress" from physics; in that field it's defined as a force that produces strain on a physi-cal body. He named our body's response to stress "general adaptation syndrome" and proposed that stress had a negative impact on physical health.

Early stress research focused on understanding how our bodies maintain a stable environment, also known as homeostasis. It explored how the mind's perception of danger caused the release of adrenaline and other hormones and how this impacted our bodies.

The experiences of soldiers in World War II led to the study of chronic stress on our psyche. Psychologist Richard Lazarus expanded on Selye's focus on physiological responses to include cognition and subsequent emotions, and the idea of coping as a mediator of the stress response. With scientific advances, the level of stress hormones could be measured under different conditions. The research revealed that certain common situations caused elevated stress hormones in everyone: novelty, unpredictability, and threat to the ego and sense of control, or NUTS.

By the 1980s, researchers began to look at the mind/body responses to stress. The concept of post-traumatic stress was expanded to include experiences of singular or continuous violence in various settings such as the home or community. During this time, new understandings of the molecular and physiological aspects of stress led to pharmacological and behavioral interventions.

In the twenty-first century, stress is now recognized as part of daily life and is widely studied across the physical and social sciences, from biology and chemistry to psychology and anthropology. This includes the study of prenatal stress, its impacts on the development of a fetus, and how this predicts health problems later in life, as well as its transgenerational effects.

The Different Types of Stress

"Stress" typically refers primarily to two types of stress, acute and chronic. You are likely to experience both types during your lifetime. The key is to recognize the difference between the two and to understand methodologies for managing both types. A proper recognition of the types of stress that you are being subjected to will aid you in ensuring that you best manage your stress and do minimal harm to your mind and body.

Along those lines, it is also important to discuss the biology of stress and how your body is equipped to respond to and adapt to it. If you understand how your body reacts during stress, you will be best prepared to minimize any long-term negative consequences. Let's look at the types of stress and what our bodies do to respond to stress within our environment.

Acute Stress

I'm guessing it wouldn't take long for you to make a list of what causes stress in your life. Let's take the commute to work. Some people have the ability to Zen out on public transit, listening to audiobooks or music, or else possess the uncanny ability to take a nap. Other people find the crowds and the noise to be disturbing. Those who drive may find themselves yelling at the other drivers in fits of road rage, whereas other people happily listen to their favorite morning talk show or podcast, or even sing along to their favorite playlist. Acute stress can also be caused by major life events such as a marriage or divorce, a new job or unemployment, and the birth of a child or loss of a loved one.

This type of stress is short-lived. The feelings associated with acute stress dissipate with removal of the stressor, or with time, or with self-management. With acute stress, your heart races, your palms get sweaty, you breathe a little faster. You may feel knots in your stomach, or you may have trouble falling asleep or staying asleep. This is a result of being flooded with cortisol and adrenaline. This can also cause you to experience a heightened sense of alertness and awareness, making you feel ready for the challenge ahead. After the situation that caused the stress has passed, your body will return to a state of calm and the levels of stress hormones will return to a state of homeostasis.

Chronic Stress

Unlike acute stress, chronic stress is omnipresent. A good example: You wake up in the morning, already stressed about the pending commute. Upon arriving at work you face a very busy day, where it feels like you can't make a dent in your to-do list. Chronic stress also occurs when dealing with a child or parent who has an illness, or when you have long-term financial woes.

During chronic stress your body is constantly flooded with hormones and there is no return to homeostasis. This is the sort of stress that causes you to have chronic insomnia and gain weight. Chronic stress contributes to the development of type 2 diabetes and cardiovascular disease, and can also cause constant muscle tension.

Common Causes of Stress

Stress is very personalized, and yet there are certain stressors that most of us have experienced at one time or another.

Work. According to the American Psychological Association, work is the leading source of stress. Modern work culture is often defined by long hours, limited vacations, and an "always on" work culture facilitated by technology.

Finances. In places around the country, the cost of living is increasing much faster than wages. Furthermore, large student loans and other household debt can strain budgets. Last, the rise of the "gig economy" means unpredictable and inconsistent income.

Home and family. If you are at work all the time, it's likely that your family isn't getting as much attention as you would like to give them. Often, even if you do have time for them, you may feel tired or distracted. Family-related stress is also dependent on what stage your family is currently experiencing. An infant can be exhausting because of the constant emotional and physical demands and the lack of sleep. Tweens and teens who are testing their independence can cause other types of chronic stress.

Health. Chronic health problems can also cause a lot of stress, especially in the United States, with its complex medical systems and high costs for treatment.

The Biology of Stress: Key Players

When it comes to stress, there is no separation between mind and body. It is unlikely that you will experience only physical symptoms and not behavioral and emotional ones or vice versa. In modern life we no longer face down predators on a regular basis. But our bodies still respond to what the brain perceives as life-threatening situations, such as a speeding car approaching when we are attempting to cross the road. Now add to this equation a 12-hour workday after very little sleep. The end result will likely be that the body will overrespond and release copious amounts of hormones, such as adrenaline (epinephrine) and cortisol.

So how does this amazing chemical reaction occur? When our bodies perceive a threatening stimulus through our eyes, ears or other organs, they send a signal to the amygdala, which is an almond-shaped cluster of neurons in the brain's temporal lobe. It's part of the limbic system, which is responsible for emotions, memories, arousal, motivation, and learning. The limbic system includes multiple parts of the brain, such as the amygdala, hypothalamus, hippocampus, and thalamus.

Amygdala

The amygdala is essential to your experience of various emotions. It also helps you perceive emotions in others and primes you to react—the fight-or-flight response—even before other parts of your brain can figure out if you need to be scared or not. When the amygdala is stimulated by a stressful event, it causes the hypothalamus to release a pituitary-adrenal stress hormone called corticotropin-releasing hormone (CPH). This hormone triggers the adrenal gland to release two other very important stress hormones: adrenaline and cortisol. The release of stress hormones is important for the regulation of our emotional, psychological, and physical responses to stimuli. Even though high levels of stress hormones can damage neural pathways, this damage is not permanent. Your brain's plasticity facilitates the regrowth and development of new pathways through various activities that increase plasticity, such as exercise.

Adrenaline

The release of adrenaline primes the body for emergency action by shifting blood flow from the skin and digestive tract to the muscles and brain and improving blood pressure and breathing. This is what many call an "adrenaline rush." It's evident by an increase in your heart rate. In the case of breathing, the hormone causes small airways in the lungs to open wide and take in more oxygen. This boost in oxygen to the brain increases alertness and heightens the senses, including enlarging the pupils of the eyes. When there is too much adrenaline, you experience heart palpitations, sweating, and rapid breathing, and it can be dangerous to your heart and other organs.

Cortisol

In moderate amounts, cortisol is part of a healthy response to stimuli. It helps restore the body to homeostasis after a stressful event by regulating blood pressure; the immune system; the metabolism of proteins, carbohydrates, and fat; and anti-inflammatory action. Under prolonged or chronic stress, the body makes more cortisol than it can process. At high levels it can impair important bodily functions, making cells become insulin resistant, for example. This causes weight gain and an increase in blood sugar, with the latter leading to type 2 diabetes. It can also shrink the prefrontal cortex and increase the size of the amygdala. This reaction makes the body more susceptible to stress, creating a vicious cycle that makes the brain remain in a near-constant state of fight or flight.

Hypothalamus

The hypothalamus links the endocrine and nervous systems through the pituitary gland, which hangs by a thin "thread" from the hypothalamus. Located at the base of the brain, the hypothalamus is also referred to as the master switchboard, because it controls the endocrine system and is key to maintaining equilibrium within the body. It does this by controlling the neural and endocrine responses to stimuli. It regulates the autonomic nervous system (heartbeat, breathing, and other involuntary actions) by stimulating or inhibiting important functions of the body—body temperature, respiration, cardiac regulation, hunger, thirst, sleep, circadian rhythms. It also regulates aspects of parenting and attachment behaviors, vasomotor activity, and blood pressure.

Key Parts of the Brain

The brain is made up of three different parts: the cerebrum, the cerebellum, and the brain stem. The cerebrum is where the brain processes stress and deploys the release of hormones within the body.

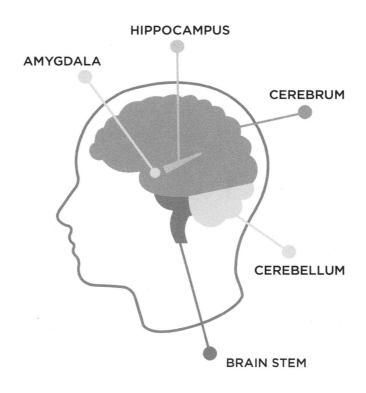

Where Stress Accumulates in the Body

When we experience stress, the brain sends hormones all over the body as part of a defense mechanism, also knowns as our "fight or flight" reflex. Over time, chronic stress can be detrimental to the body, causing harm to the different organs and systems.

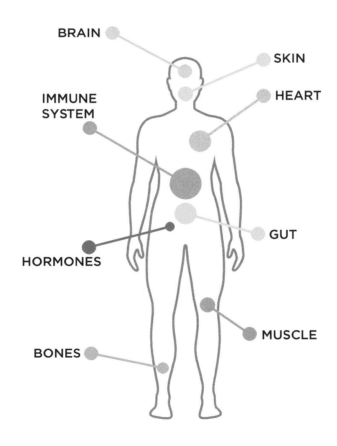

Prefrontal Cortex

Another part of the brain involved in the stress response is the prefrontal cortex. It's the most evolved part of the brain and is responsible for advanced cognitive processes. Rational decisions start here. Interestingly, this part of the brain isn't fully developed until humans reach their mid-twenties, which explains why teenagers tend to engage in risky behavior and make question-able choices.

The Signs and Symptoms of Unproductive Stress Relief

As you have learned, acute and chronic stresses initiate a series of physical, emotional, and psycho-logical reactions that are based in neural responses to stimuli. However, with the right strategies you can intervene and slow down or prevent the domino effect that leads to negative impacts on our health. But first let's discuss some of the responses to stress and how they manifest in our daily lives.

Fatigue and Tension

In a situation of acute stress, after the body has responded, it takes about a half hour for the physical and emotional reactions to dissipate, as the hormones fade away. However, if there is chronic stress, then the body stays primed, and you begin to feel exhausted. All that physical and mental alertness created by rapid heartbeat and breathing, plus the increase in blood pressure, can lead to fatigue. It is like being at the starting line of a race waiting for the gun, but it never goes off. Eventually you tire from this heightened physical reaction, but your muscles remain tense as they wait for that moment to go into action. Because the stress does not go away, neither does the tension. It can show up as headaches, tense muscles in the shoulders and neck, or teeth grinding.

Sleeplessness

Regardless of the source of stress, a state of heightened awareness triggered by adrenaline makes it difficult to relax so that you can fall asleep. For example, a conflict in a relationship with a friend or family member that isn't resolved before heading to bed makes it difficult to fall asleep or stay asleep. In the short and long term,

lack of sleep will impair mental and physical func-
tioning and leave you even less prepared to deal
with stress.

Depression and Anxiety

Chronic stress can cause depression and anxiety
when you feel overwhelmed by circumstances you
face. For example, if you are experiencing financial
difficulties and you don't have a means to increase
your income, you may become depressed or anxious. A simple task such as going to the mailbox,
where you know late notices will be waiting for you,
can further fuel these feelings. Furthermore, lack of
sleep can trigger depression and anxiety, and at the
same time, depression and anxiety can trigger lack
of sleep. Good sleep hygiene—daily habits that train
your body to sleep—is an important part of building
emotional resilience.

Weight Gain and Weight Loss

Too much cortisol can lead to insulin resistance.
An excess of insulin in the body leads to more fat
storage in your cells, which results in weight gain.
The hypothalamus regulates the body's system of

homeostasis and can inhibit or stimulate hunger or thirst, depending on your body's needs. For many people, stress causes them to have an increase in appetite, also known as stress eating. People typically find comfort in high-fat, high-salt, or high-sugar foods such as potato chips or ice cream. Combine stress eating with insulin resistance and a slowed metabolism, and it's easy to see how stress can lead to weight gain. Conversely, some people have a reduced appetite when stressed, which leads to weight loss.

Chronic and Serious Illness

It is not hard to understand why people with chronic and serious illnesses may feel stressed. But being stressed can also cause chronic and serious illnesses. As discussed earlier, flooding the body with cortisol and adrenaline can lead to a number of health issues. Inflammation and reduced immunity can lead to chronic and serious illnesses like diabetes (from insulin resistance caused by too much cortisol), hypertension (from high levels of adrenaline), and cardiovascular disease.

Before You Begin

This book is going to help you face the stressful situations of your life by providing tools to manage your physical, emotional, and psychological responses. Some of these strategies will be your conscious responses to an in-the-moment experience of a stressful event. Others will help you build your resilience to stress by being physically and emotionally fit to face daily challenges and more intense unexpected experiences. For example, if you are about to lead an important meeting and feel your heart racing and your hands sweating, a long deep breath can slow down your pulse and get you calm and confident enough to make a big impression.

If you want to deploy a long-term strategy for dealing with stress on a daily basis, developing a practice of mindfulness is key. This may include walking or any type of consistent exercise routine. The goal is to keep your body ready to deal with whatever comes your way without risking your mental and physical health. If you are experiencing a difficult time in your life, such as a divorce or unemployment or the death of a loved one, these approaches can help you get through to the other side.

Many of the actions that this book will prescribe will require you to have pen and paper ready to do your writing "homework," so it is good to have a journal to complete writing prompts. To make it special, you may want to buy a particular pen just for this process, as you get ready for chapters 2 through 6.

Chapter 2

Enduring Everyday Hassles

For most of us, it's not the big stuff that gets us stressed but the endless demands of daily life. Yes, our brains are hardwired to react to the real danger that a lion or a fire would present, but it seems to behave the same way when we are stuck in traffic trying to get to and from work—on the daily.

Hectic Commute

Most likely you are all too familiar with a hectic morning and evening commute to and from work. You've experienced the stress of setting out early only to hit the freeway and find yourself sitting in a parking lot. And as much as you try to stay calm, you find yourself checking the time and hoping you won't be late.

 ## Exercise: Mindfulness

So what can you do the next time someone cuts you off or speeds up so you can't merge, even though you've been indicating a lane change with your blinker for a while? Perhaps you could try mindfulness. Let's start with your breath. The respiratory system is impacted by stress, and rapid, shallow breathing is often an early sign that you've reached your emotional and mental limit. The goal is to focus on your body as you breathe.

1. Sit upright in your seat and on a count of five breathe in slowly through your nose.
2. On a count of five, blow out through your mouth.

3. While you breathe in, focus on feeling your breath go up through your nose and into your lungs. Focus on the expansion of your diaphragm as your body fills with air; give attention to your diaphragm as it deflates when the breath flows out.
4. Do this five times until you feel your body calming down.

The second mindfulness exercise that is useful—while still allowing you to pay attention to your driving—is to focus on a mantra. A mantra is a word or sound that you can repeat to help you get into a meditative state. It works by replacing ruminating negative thoughts with a more calming phrase. Usually you'd close your eyes to help you "check out" from the world around you and focus inward, but please don't do that while you drive. Instead, this mantra will help you relax and be calm, so road rage stays far away from your mind.

1. Any word or phrase will work as a mantra. Perhaps, "I get there when I get there."
2. Repeat the phrase for at least five minutes and for as long as you need to.

Too Many Deadlines

Deadlines aren't just the domain of the busy executive with a long list of deliverables and a staff to support, guide, and inspire. Deadlines also impact the student who has to deal with the competing demands of midterms or finals, or the stay-at-home parent who has to manage finances and kids' schedules. Whatever your situation, having too many deadlines can make you feel as if there is no way you can get it all done unless you find a way to be in two places at once.

 ## Exercise: Writing

Writing is a great way to get rid of worries by placing them on the page. Writing can inspire greatness in you because articulating concrete plans for your dreams and desires is the first step in making them come true.

This writing exercise demonstrates how to connect with your emotions and how to prioritize and celebrate what you accomplish. For this exercise, you will need a calendar to schedule your commitments. You'll also need a journal to write down your feelings.

1. On the first page of your journal, make a list of everything you have to do in the next

month, along with due dates, and enter those on the calendar.

2. Once everything is entered in the calendar, take a minute to think about how this makes you feel; write down three words that describe those feelings on the bottom of the list.

3. Below the list, write down what you have to do in the next week and the days/times that everything is due.

4. Analyze the list; which things are actually not that important and can be deleted, and which things can be delayed for a few days?

5. For the items that don't need immediate attention, strike a line through them. Poof! Your list is now shorter.

6. Take a moment to write down three words that describe how you feel now that you have a shorter list.

7. For those tasks that can be delayed, write a date/time within the following weeks when you can take action, or take it a step farther and rank the top five priorities of the week.

8. As you complete each activity or task, put a check mark next to the item. Note the date and time and put a word of celebration next to each item when done.

Bedtime Struggles with Your Toddler

Anyone who has ever taken care of a toddler knows how exhausting that can be. Toddlers are discovering their autonomy and asserting their identity and want very much to get their own way. And one of the times that they *love* to express their independence is bedtime. Even as adults we delay our bedtime for TV, social media, or emails that could wait until the morning, so it's easy to understand your two-year-old's point of view, right?

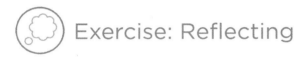 ## Exercise: Reflecting

One way to shift the stress of the toddler bedtime is to shift your thinking about your toddler. What are they doing? Playing? Being defiant? This is part of the development stage for any toddler. When you understand it's part of their growth, you can begin to look at this power struggle in a very different way. This doesn't mean bedtime will miraculously get any easier, but it won't be as emotionally exhausting as it could otherwise be.

1. First, think about how much you love your toddler—the amazing human being that you are so excited to see grow and develop.
2. Remind yourself constantly of that love in those moments of resistance that are driving you up the wall.
3. To keep focused on that love, be sure to tell your toddler how much you love them as you go through the bedtime routine.
4. Shift your mindset to think about how you are helping your child grow and develop during this particular struggle. Doing so helps to teach them discipline and routine in their life.
5. You will find that staying focused on the love that you have for that little person shifts the bedtime routine from a moment of just another struggle to the opportunity to think, feel, and show love to your child.

Homework Battles

I am in my 50s, and still remember how much I did not want to do homework when I was a child. Instead, I wanted to watch TV. And although my daughter is in her 20s, I also viscerally remember what it meant to ensure that her homework was done on time. Any struggle with a child requires a mindset that is calm, focused, and controlled. There is no point in getting angry, yelling, or using punishment to get your child to do something they don't want to do. By the time it is all over you will both be upset and drained.

Exercise: Mindfulness

Use this mindfulness exercise to help you both relax and focus, so you two can collaborate on the intellectual challenge that is before you. It will also create a homework routine that starts out in a place of peace and not a place of conflict.

1. Together, choose several pieces of music that will become a homework playlist. Save the songs in your favorite music app. Another option is to stream music of a particular type, which you can label as your "homework channel."
2. Choose something that soothes and calms, such as classical, new-age, or jazz.
3. Before your child starts working on the assignment, both of you should listen to the music for at least five minutes (set the timer on your phone).
4. Hold hands, and close your eyes.
5. Try to identify the instruments that are being played or focus on the meaning of the words being said.
6. After listening together for five minutes, keep the music playing while your child does their homework and you do whatever it is that you have dedicated "homework" time to doing.

Dinner on the Table

For many working people, getting dinner on the table often means picking up something on the way home or having something delivered. It's costly but also a lot less stressful than trying to remember what is in the refrigerator while making your way home from a busy day so you can make a hot meal for your family. But cooking weeknight dinners doesn't have to be hectic and harried.

 ## Exercise: Writing

This exercise focuses on creating food combinations that get you excited about dinnertime instead of feeling anxious about it. Spending a little time on meal planning can help you feel more in control of what can be a stressful task of daily life.

1. In a journal or a notebook, write down the ingredients you have in your fridge and cupboard.
2. Think about what it is that you want to make for dinner.

3. Write down three items you have in your fridge that could be the feature of your meal. It may be easiest to feature a protein, but really anything can be the main item of your meal.
4. Choose only one item that you want to make for dinner that day.
5. In a few sentences, describe how you want to cook that main course—e.g., bake it, fry it, or steam it.
6. Make a list of the ingredients that you want to use to season your main course and write out the steps you will take to prepare the item for cooking.
7. Make a list of two side dishes that you want to add to your meal and how you will prepare them.

When you've completed these steps you're ready to make dinner, and instead of it being overwhelming, you now have a plan.

Household Chores

Getting the chores done is one of those adulting things that we all have to do, because the bathroom or laundry won't clean or wash itself. Since that's the case, you may as well have fun doing them by using this opportunity for movement to your advantage.

 ## Exercise: Movement

This exercise is going to get you moving and put you in a happy mindset instead of dread about cleaning. By the time you are done with all your chores you will be in a happy space, because your house will be cleaner and tidier, and you'll have completed the chores while listening to music that you love. Plus, you'll have added more than a few steps to your daily count. You're welcome.

1. Begin by putting on your favorite dance music, whatever it is that gets you smiling, happy, and ready to move your hips and feet.

2. Grab the vacuum, broom, mop, or duster and make it your partner as you proceed to dance and get it done.

3. Imagine you are dancing with your celebrity crush.

4. Whenever you have completed your mopping/sweeping/vacuuming with a dance routine that has you feeling like you are ready for *Dancing with the Stars*, do a celebratory dance.

5. Take a spin around the room to the next song that starts, and when it is done it will be time to start chore number two.

6. When it is time to clean the bathroom, scrub that bathtub or the toilet to the rhythm of the beat while you sing along.

7. Do the same with the kitchen, etc., while making sure to do a dance in between each chore.

Kid Logistics

Gone are the days when children spent after-school hours playing in parks, playgrounds, and backyards, or even hanging out at home watching their favorite show. These days, many children have a calendar filled with activities that require them to be in more places than their parents. Of course, one of the ways to reduce this stressor is to reduce the number of activities that children are involved in. But regardless of the number of activities they have, the logistics of the where, when, and how can get even more complicated if there is more than one child.

 ## Exercise: Mindfulness

When the very thought of your child's after-school and weekend activities has you feeling overwhelmed, it is time for a mindfulness exercise. This practice is designed to get you in a calm and centered space, so that traffic, forgotten gear, or even a child's meltdown can't get to you.

1. Start with being still; it doesn't matter if you are standing, sitting, or lying down.
2. Take a pause for five minutes (set the timer on your phone, which you should place on Do Not Disturb mode).
3. Close your eyes and take a long, deep breath through your nose and exhale through your mouth. Imagine a beautiful place in a natural setting that you went to and loved, or someplace you have never been but dream of visiting.
4. Picture yourself there, taking a long, slow walk and enjoying the beauty all around you. Look around and notice the colors and the smells and feel the sense of calm.
5. Picture yourself finding a place to sit within the imaginary scene and focus on one thing in the scene. Do this until the timer goes off.

When the alarm goes off, open your eyes. You will feel a sense of peace and revitalization from the little vacation you took in your mind.

Coworker Challenges

If you've never experienced working with a difficult person, consider yourself lucky. A challenging
coworker can make the difference between waking
up with a smile on your face, excited for the day
ahead, and waking up with a sense of dread and
anxiety about what's to come.

 ## Exercise: Writing

The goal of this exercise is to focus on the positive
elements of your job. It's a reminder of all the wonderful things about the work and the wonderful
people you work with, in spite of that challenging
coworker. After you complete this exercise, that
difficult coworker will no longer be the focus of your
attention. You'll feel empowered to deal with them
because you'll know that they are a minor downside
to a whole lot of upside.

1. In your journal, start a new page with the header "Why I Love My Job."
2. Write down the following sentences and fill in the blank for each of them:
   - "I applied for this job because _____."
   - "I was happy I got this job because I wanted to _____."
   - "I love going to work every day because _____."
   - "My favorite person at work is _____ because he/she/they _____."
   - "Today I am excited to go to work because I look forward to _____."

3. When you have completed the last sentence, go back to the beginning and read over what you have written.
4. Repeat one more time.
5. Now go to work (or back to work, depending on when you are doing this) and get it done.

Chapter 3

Conquering New Experiences

Having new experiences is a part of life. From the time we are born, no two days are exactly the same. As you age, it's fair to say that you'll experience a number of life-defining transitions that will be both exciting and scary—and sometimes both at once. Rarely do we escape these events, but what's more important is to focus on how you manage them from an emotional perspective.

Starting a New Job

One of the more exciting moments in your life may include when you finally got that job you put so much energy into applying and interviewing for. *Woo-hoo!* But once the celebration is over, reality sets in, along with anxiety over meeting new people and learning new job duties. Sure, you're still excited, but you may start to feel a little nervous. In fact, you may feel anxious for a while, until you get the hang of everything.

 ## Exercise: Mindfulness

One of the best ways to achieve psychological and emotional calm is by integrating a daily meditative practice into your morning routine. It is emotionally and mentally fortifying to start your day with a sense of calm, mental clarity, and focus. It not only helps you be more productive, but it builds resilience for the stress of whatever unexpected tasks may come your way during the day. You can also repeat it at lunchtime as a booster shot to get you through the rest of the day.

This exercise will also include affirmations, statements you say out loud (or, depending on where you are, in your head) that describe a feeling you aspire toward. It can be as general as "I will be awesome at work today" or more specific, such as "I will close at least one deal today."

1. First, think of what phrase you'd like your affirmation to be.
2. Sit on the floor (or in your chair, at your workspace) with your legs crossed and your hands on your thighs, with your palms facing upward, in what is known as a lotus pose.
3. Close your eyes and take in a deep breath through your nose and out through your mouth.
4. Keep breathing deeply and repeat your affirmation 10 times.
5. At the last affirmation, take one final deep breath in through your nose and exhale through your mouth.
6. Open your eyes and begin your day.

I promise you a daily meditation routine will alter the way you experience the challenges of the day.

Buying a New Home

Congratulations on your new home! I'm sure you're more than ready to put your design skills to work and arrange all of the rooms just the way you want. But I bet you're feeling some stress as well about getting utilities connected and meeting new neighbors, not to mention learning to adjust to a new environment.

 ## Exercise: Writing

Transitions are a great time to write. In doing so, you can express how you feel, what you look forward to, and what you're happy to have left behind. This writing exercise will create something of a text-based vision board as you put your dreams to paper.

In your journal, write about why you chose this place as your new home.

- What in the listing got your attention?
- What on the tour did you find interesting?
- Do you have dreams for this home?

    - What kinds of activities do you want to do at your new home?
    - What memories do you want to create?
    - Whom do you envision coming over?

- Are there any changes you want to make in the future?

    - Would you like to renovate a bedroom or bathroom or a kitchen?
    - Do you have a dream shed in mind?
    - Do you want to rearrange the landscape?
    - Would you like to expand?

This writing exercise will connect you to your home and will focus you on what makes this house a home. What you write can also serve as a map for the future of your home.

Retiring

The day has finally arrived; you no longer have to get up on Monday morning to go to work. Hallelujah! You also may be feeling trepidation about the huge adjustment that comes with not doing what has dictated the rhythm of your life for the past four to five decades. So what to do with all that time? An exercise routine is as good an activity as any to get started on the rest of your life.

Exercise: Movement

Let's take advantage of all that extra time and get your body moving. A good way to start and end the day is to stretch the whole body. Stretching can keep you feeling limber and ready for the day's activities and help you relax in the evening, before bed. Stretching is also a good way to keep you flexible and strong as you get older and help prevent falls and breaks. (Please note that if you are new to a stretching routine and have any physical limitations or injuries, you should consult with your health care provider before beginning.)

1. Stand with your feet squarely planted at shoulder width.
2. Stretch your arms as far above your head as you can reach, bringing your palms together.
3. Take three deep breaths in through your nose and out through your mouth.
4. Next, drop your right arm to your side, keep your left arm close to your head, and reach over as far as you can to your right, bending at the waist; take three deep breaths.
5. Repeat by bringing your left arm to your side and bringing your right arm close to your head and reaching over as far as you can to your left; take three deep breaths.
6. Return to center with your arms above your head again; take three deep breaths.
7. Relax.

You should feel calm and centered, and your body should feel limber.

Starting College

Beginning a new academic journey can bring on a mixture of emotions. It's exciting to think about all that you will learn and the people you will meet. It can also be anxiety provoking for the same reasons. Whatever your emotion, college is a challenging proposition. Staying focused, motivated, and calm is an important aspect of getting all of your assignments done in a timely manner without losing your head.

 ## Exercise: Mindfulness

A mindfulness activity is an excellent way to feel centered and ready to slay that college dragon. You can return to this activity when the demands of school have you feeling anxious or overwhelmed. This exercise will help you improve your focus while at the same time providing a mental checkout when you need a break. You can do this counting exercise at any time and anywhere.

1. Find a quiet place that won't have too many distractions.
2. Stand with your feet shoulder width apart.
3. Close your eyes and take a long, slow, deep breath in through your nose and blow it out slowly through your mouth. Count slowly by fives until you reach 100. (If you really want to get your focus on, try counting by threes.)
4. When you have completed your slow count to 100, open your eyes and get back to what you need to do, taking advantage of your improved focus.

This exercise requires you to ignore what is going on with you and focus on counting. It is also a great way to prepare your brain for a challenging task.

Getting Married

Here's to a long life together filled with love, joy, and happiness. This is an exciting start to a new phase in your life. Even if you've been married before, or if you've already been cohabiting, this is a new status that may change the way you interact with your partner.

 ## Exercise: Writing

A new chapter in life is a great time to write down your dreams and your hopes for the future. This can include new activities you want to do and even a new approach or disposition toward life. This exercise is designed to help you face forward with loving and positive feelings, instead of anxiety about what comes next.

1. With your partner, write down how you see your life together.

   o What are you excited about?
   o What are you afraid of?
   o What expectations do you have for your behavior and that of your partner? For example, who will be doing what chores?

2. Next, write down how you envision your life together in a year.

   ○ Will you be living at the same address?
   ○ Do you plan to have children, or do you want to get a pet?

3. What about your long-term plans? What does your married life look like five years from now?

   ○ Will you have traveled to one of your bucket-list destinations?
   ○ Will it be time for another child or a new car?

4. Consider what life with your new spouse will be like 10 years from now.

   ○ Will you have created some new family traditions or rituals that reflect your values?
   ○ What countries will you have visited together?

Moving to a New City

So, you got that new job and now you are moving to a new city—where you may or may not have any friends. No matter the reason you're pulling up stakes, moving is a stressful experience. There's all of the packing and unpacking, plus other tedious tasks associated with a move.

 ## Exercise: Reflecting

It's understandable that you may want to simply curl up in bed, pull the blankets over your head, and hope the whole thing can get done without you. But sadly, even if you have delegated the packing and heavy lifting to professionals, they still need you to direct the process. The challenge here is to get yourself in the right frame of mind—that is, to start and end the day in a state of calm. Remember that the way you think changes the way you feel.

- Shift your perspective from a negativity bias to a positivity bias.
- Focus on all that could go right instead of focusing on what could possibly go wrong. Things will go wrong, but there is no point worrying about them.
- If you are in a positive state of mind, problem-solving will be easier than if you participate in disaster thinking.
- Think of this move as a new adventure that will bring personal and professional growth, instead of new people and places you must get to know. This will make your move a much easier—and more enjoyable—transition.

Changing Careers

If you've successfully marketed yourself in a new field and have a new career to develop, then you have a lot to be proud of. This is not an easy task, so go you! Although feeling a little afraid is a perfectly normal emotion for this stage of your life, let's make sure that fear isn't your constant companion.

Exercise: Mindfulness

The mental commitment required to learn a new role in a new field can make you feel as if you have no time for anything else. But making time for mindfulness will boost your mental clarity, focus, creativity, and productivity—wonderful things to help you slay at that new career. This exercise is something you can do at your workplace that will increase your efficiency and productivity.

This mindfulness practice should last for at least 20 minutes. That means no phone calls or email. You can open your phone or computer to a mindfulness or meditation website if you'd prefer a guided practice.

Set the timer on your phone for 20 minutes.

1. Think of a mantra that will help you focus on succeeding in your new career.
2. Turn your phone facedown on your desk or table, or better yet, put it away and set the Do Not Disturb function (if you have an assistant who manages your calls, ask him or her to take a message for the next 20 minutes). If you don't have a private desk, consider booking a conference room or break room, if possible.
3. If you're doing this without guided prompts, put on earphones or play music if it helps you focus.
4. Now get to work; start repeating your mantra. Remember to bring your focus back to your mantra if your mind wanders.
5. At the end of 20 minutes, take five minutes to walk around to get your blood circulating and give your brain some time to reboot.
6. Use this time to get rehydrated with some fluids or take a bathroom break. It would also give your mind a boost if you went outside and got some fresh air for a few minutes.

Breaking Up

The song lyrics are correct: "Breaking up is hard to do." To be blunt, this applies whether you're the one doing the dumping or you're the one getting dumped. To get you through this difficult time, it's good practice to turn to writing as therapy.

 ## Exercise: Writing

To clear your mind and soothe your heart, engage in a writing exercise that puts your relationship in perspective. Writing down your thoughts can help you remain open and willing to give love another chance in the future. You are probably caught up in your feelings, replaying certain moments in your head as you ruminate on where you went wrong in your relationship. This exercise will take you from your heart to your head, by providing systematic analysis on your relationship that hopefully brings closure and helps make sense of what happened.

1. Think about everything that went right in your relationship; write at least one page that outlines all the good things and good times. (Yes, *at least* one page.)

   Focus on the dynamics of the relationship. Think about what you both did that made the relationship enjoyable, rewarding, and fulfilling, and write it all down. This may be difficult and somewhat counterproductive, but the purpose of the exercise is to help you make sense of your decision to spend time with this person. It also helps you focus on the good of the relationship without getting drowned in all that went wrong, and decreases opportunities to beat yourself up for making what you think was the wrong choice.

BREAKING UP *continues*

2. Now think about what went wrong in the relationship and fill no more than two pages in your notebook or journal. It is important to limit your pages here because it's too easy to get sucked into the negativity. Try not to focus on what's wrong with the person you were with, but rather focus on what *you* did wrong. Focus on the dynamics of the relationship; reflect on who you were in that relationship.

3. Once those two lists are complete, it's time to think about the future. List the characteristics of your latest relationship that you would choose to take and that you would choose to leave behind. Use no more than one page for each.

4. Lastly, focus on what you'd change in a future relationship. At the top of a page write: "What I Will Do Differently Next Time." On that page, write down any actions you plan to take to improve your chance of finding a long-lasting relationship. This can include reading self-help books or going to therapy.

By the time you are done with this process, you will appreciate the place this relationship has in the journey of your life. Hopefully, you will have also learned some more about who you are, what you do and don't want in a relationship, and how to do your love life better next time.

Chapter 4

Managing Ongoing Issues

Sometimes life throws you a curveball. Oftentimes, you're able to catch it and keep moving forward. At other times, it is not so easy to put a stressor behind you. These types of challenges include caring for an elderly parent, feeling financially insecure, or raising a child with chronic health issues or special needs. They could also include dealing with a boss at work who has you wanting to quit. Each of these challenges can result in stress that must be managed in a healthy way.

Caring for Elderly Parents

As we get older, so do our parents. If we are lucky, they will remain healthy, active, self-sufficient, and able to enjoy their post-retirement life. For others, life takes its toll and our parents require some support to get through the day. This may be as simple as a housekeeper who cooks and runs errands, or more significant, such as finding a full-time caregiver (which may be you) to provide round-the-clock assistance.

The role reversal can be challenging for any parent. It must be sobering to realize your child needs to care for you instead of the other way around. What's more, the responsibility and obligation children feel toward their parents may make it seem like no matter what they do, it is never enough.

 ## Exercise: Movement

The following movement exercise is designed to help you deal with the anxiety of watching a parent age and need help or care. A good workout can make you feel as if you have achieved something, plus you feel great after. If you already have an exercise routine, then you already have an outlet. You may add this to your exercise/movement routine on a regular basis to get the most out of the activity.

1. For this exercise, all you need are comfortable shoes and clothes, and the right outerwear that will allow you to face the elements no matter what they are.
2. Take a walk outside, no matter the weather. This walk is not geared toward fitness but is instead focused on a mood boost and mental clarity.
3. Make the walk at a brisk pace, with a goal of walking for a minimum of 15 minutes.
4. On some days this amount of time will do the trick. Other times you may need to walk for an hour just to get yourself into a place of contentment.

Feeling Financially Insecure

Not having enough money to pay your bills and maintain your life is enough to keep you awake at night and ruminating all day. It's difficult not to have money on your mind when you are preoccupied with how to get more of it.

 ## Exercise: Writing

This writing exercise is about problem-solving and making a plan that will provide some direction and hope when it comes to your long-term financial health.

1. Write down the financial dreams and desires that you have in the short term (the next three months).
2. Do the same for the long term (one to five years). Some things to consider include:
   - Do you want to buy a home?
   - Would you like to move to a new neighborhood?
   - Do you want to take a dream vacation?
   - Do you want to start a retirement fund for yourself?

3. Once you've logged your goals, write down how you can achieve these dreams. The possibilities include:
   - a raise
   - a new job with a higher pay scale
   - a side job to catch up on bills or to create an emergency fund
   - reducing the size of your home so you can reduce spending and be more financially secure

4. Next, pick one of your financial dreams from step 1 and connect it to one or more of your money management strategies from step 3.

FEELING FINANCIALLY INSECURE *continues*

5. The final steps will include making a short list of five clearly stated goals that will allow you to implement one of those management strategies. For each step, add a due date that will keep you on track for reaching at least one of your financial goals.

    ○ For example, if you decide to ask for a raise, you will want to articulate at least three reasons why you deserve one. What have you contributed to your organization? When did you go above and beyond expectations? Or perhaps you have done your research and found that you are underpaid with regard to the median salary in your field.

    ○ If your strategy is to find a side job, then make a short list of jobs that you can do: walking dogs, house-sitting, assisting with errands, retail, customer service, etc. Then create profiles on the relevant online employment platforms such as TaskRabbit, Wag!, Indeed, etc., and start looking.

Living in an Unhappy Marriage/Relationship

If you're in an unhappy marriage or relationship, likely you're debating how much you should endure before calling it quits. Maybe you've decided to stay and aren't sure how to change things for the better. In an unhappy marriage it's easy for the good in your life to get overshadowed by the challenges that come from sharing physical and emotional space with someone who doesn't bring you joy.

 Exercise: Writing

Until you decide what to do about your marriage, don't let the relationship dictate all of the happiness in your life. Happiness is a way of being. Your life doesn't have to be "good" for you to be happy. Making a conscious decision to be thankful has its payoffs. Research has shown that people who express gratitude experience less stress. Being grateful also lets you focus on the positive, which can push the "bad" in your life out of view.

1. Complete the following prompts on a series of index cards, one for each sentence. You can provide several answers for each prompt:

   - When I think about my family I am grateful for:
   - When I think about my work I am grateful for:
   - I am grateful for the opportunity to create:
   - When I think about my home I am grateful for:
   - When I think about my health I am grateful for:
   - When I think about my finances I am grateful for:
   - Overall I am grateful for:

2. When you have completed these cards, staple, clip, or wrap them with a rubber band, and put them in a bag that you carry every day.
3. Anytime you are feeling down, check back with your list and let it shift your perspective and lift your spirits.

Feeling Lonely

Despite all the virtual connections that social media provides, loneliness is on the rise. Even though Facebook and Instagram or a WhatsApp group can keep you up-to-date with the goings-on of your family and friends, or your favorite celebrity, humans still crave real-life interaction. Furthermore, with so many people working remotely, many of us (me included) spend our workdays at home alone in our pajamas.

 Exercise: Movement

To help you maintain a connection with people, let's focus on movement. Find at least one group of people who engage in a physical activity that you enjoy. Your choice of group activity may be anything from a Meetup group of walkers, to a salsa class at your local YMCA, to a biking club sponsored by a nearby bike shop, to a hike with your regional Sierra Club.

1. Think of three physical activities that you enjoy.
2. Use the Internet to find out which organizations offer the kinds of activities on your list. For example, if yoga is on your list, finding a class nearby should be easy.
3. If classes aren't your speed, try the online Meetup platform to see what groups already exist in your area. For example, there are hiking groups and tennis groups, or maybe Ultimate Frisbee is more your speed.
4. Whatever activity you choose, it's a great way to connect with people who have similar interests as you and provides a foundation for interaction.
5. Even if you don't make friends, the camaraderie you experience will relieve you of some of your loneliness. Plus, the good feeling that comes from doing what you enjoy is a bonus.
6. If all that is not enough you may also find satisfaction and accomplishment in your improved muscular and cardiovascular fitness.

Caring for a Special Needs Child

Raising children is hard. Raising a child with special needs is extra hard. The degree to which you feel stressed will depend on how much care your child needs. How much support you get from your network of friends and family and community-based resources is also a factor. Regardless of your situation, it's easy to carry your stress in your neck and shoulders, which can lead to headaches, chronic pain, stiffness, soreness, and reduced range of motion.

 ## Exercise: Movement

This movement activity is focused on helping you release some of the tension from your neck, shoulders, and upper back. You can do this exercise while sitting, but I suggest you stand, because most of us spend way too much time sitting as it is. Standing can also better facilitate blood circulation.

1. While standing, relax your shoulders and loosely hang your arms by your sides with your open palms facing forward. (If you are sitting, then place your palms upward on your thighs.)
2. Lift your shoulders straight up toward your ears.
3. Using a circular motion, roll your shoulders backward, then downward, then forward, and then back up toward your ears.
4. Slowly repeat step 3 five times.
5. Then, using a similar motion, roll your shoulders in the opposite direction, starting forward, then rolling downward toward your back, and then back up to your shoulders.
6. Slowly repeat step 5 five times.
7. Relax your shoulders.
8. Last, breathe in slowly through your nose while gradually raising your shoulders upward toward your ears, then slowly breathe out as you relax your shoulders back down at the same pace.
9. Repeat step 8 five times.

Having a Partner with Mental Health Issues

When we love someone it is really hard to see them struggle with mental health issues. Being in a close and intimate relationship with someone who has a mental illness can be emotionally and psychologically demanding. The unexpected and unpredictable behaviors and emotions that may be a feature of their mental health issue make it challenging to connect. What makes it hard to live with someone with a mental health issue is that their behavior and emotions do not necessarily reflect who they really are or what they really feel. Rather, their actions and feelings are the result of the mental health issue they struggle with.

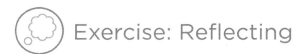 ## Exercise: Reflecting

To be on the receiving end of emotional turmoil requires a lot of patience. To actively love the person behind the illness requires a shift in perspective that separates them from their behavior. Focusing on what you like and love about them is key. Telling them is even more important. This exercise is really about focusing on the positive. When your partner is having symptoms that may make you frustrated or angry or hurt, remind yourself about good times you have had in the recent past. I can't promise it will make things easy, but it may serve as a way to focus on your connection when it is hard to think about the love you share.

1. Think of some good times between the two of you. The more recent the moment, the better, because it will make you cogni-zant that good times are still possible now and in the future. If you choose a moment in the distant past, it may make you think about all that you have lost instead of all that you have now.
2. Share this moment with your partner to also get them shifted to thinking about the good times you have had together. They may not be ready to hear it in the moment, and if they aren't, focus on your own think-ing and less on theirs.

You may find that communicating these positive aspects of your relationship and your partner's personality is just what they need to focus on being well. It can also provide optimism about the future and make them feel loved at a time when they may not feel worthy of that love.

Dealing with a Chronic Illness

Living with a chronic illness such as diabetes, cancer, or multiple sclerosis can be very stressful. It can shift the focus from enjoying the day-to-day moments in life to struggling to be as well as possible. Managing your illness may require scheduled medications or medical interventions. Perhaps your illness is one you simply endure. No matter your physical limitations, feeling "able" helps you develop a good relationship with your body. Movement builds physical strength and stamina. It may also reduce the severity and frequency of symptoms—depending on the kind of illness you may have. Last, movement can cause the brain to release the pleasure chemicals of serotonin and dopamine.

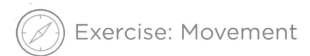 Exercise: Movement

The focus of this movement exercise is to move for at least 10 minutes. (Make sure to consult with your health care provider to make sure that you choose a form of exercise that is right for you.) You can perform this exercise at any time of the day.

- Walking is a great choice because it does not require a lot of equipment or skill, plus it can be done anywhere and at any time. If walking is a challenge due to physical limitations, consult with your health care provider about options that are right for you.
- Another great option is swimming. Moving in water is often easier and more effective at building strength than moving on land. Water provides a natural resistance as well as buoyancy that reduces the impact on joints.
- If you do not know how to swim and are physically able, learning this lifesaving skill will allow you to focus on the strength and capability of your body rather than its limitations.
- If swimming is not an option, perhaps sign up for a movement class that takes place in water. Make sure to ask for a free test-run class before you commit in case you find it difficult to do or to fit into your life's routine.

Chapter 5

Navigating Life-Changing Events

Major life events are those that change who we are and how we see ourselves. These are the moments where we experience intense emotion—a loved one's death, job loss, or displacement from a natural disaster. These major life events catch us off guard and change our lives in some significant way.

Birth or Adoption of a Child

Congratulations on the new addition to your family! After all the planning and waiting, the day is finally here, and your joy can't be contained. However, amid your joy, it's perfectly normal to feel over-whelmed as you adjust to this new person in your life. The change in your day-to-day schedule and additional expenses while you're creating a bond with your child, someone you'll love uncondition-ally and forever, are a lot to consider. Finding a healthy way to deal with the stress of being a new parent is vital.

 Exercise: Writing

Journaling about your thoughts, feelings, and adventures with your child creates a memory for you as a parent, while also providing you with a place to dump your anxieties.

Before you begin, think about whether you want to share this with your child in the future or if it is something just for you. That decision may shape what you write about. Whatever you decide, I encourage you to give some structure to your entries that will help you really get at whatever it is that is on your mind on a daily basis.

You may use whatever format you choose, but in the event you are challenged by not knowing where to start, I offer the following as a suggested outline for your entries:

What happened today. Simply list memorable events that occurred in whatever way you like.

What I did about it. Your reaction to whatever happened today is the focus of this section because you want to focus on your actions.

How I feel about it. Parenting is emotional, and naming your feelings will help you understand who you are as a parent while getting your emotions out before you go to bed. This will help you free your mind and help you sleep.

What I learned about my child or myself as a parent today. Seeing the lesson in the everyday gives meaning to the mundane as well as the exciting parenting moments, and to your life in general. It reframes how you view these moments.

What I would do the same or differently. Well, there is no point learning a lesson if you don't change what you do. Applying the daily lessons—whether big or small—will not only improve your parenting but also provide an opportunity for personal growth.

Death of a Parent

Grief is a challenging experience that we all go through, and the loss of a parent is no different. No matter the nature of your relationship, the loss of a parent is often a turning point. It's one of those moments that mark a before-and-after in the story of your life. For some people the grief they experience is all-consuming and never-ending. Others find that moving forward and living each day to the fullest is the best way to honor their parent. Either way is okay, it just depends on the person who is experiencing the loss.

 Exercise: Writing

It's important to know that there is no wrong or right way to grieve the loss of a parent. However, there is a widely respected model that maps out the stages of grief. In this model, developed by Elisabeth Kübler-Ross, people experience, in order, denial, anger, bargaining, depression, and acceptance. Before we begin the writing exercise, let's get a basic understanding of these stages so that you can organize your thoughts and work through your feelings.

Denial. This is the result of the shock you first feel when death comes, even if your parent was elderly or ill and it was something you expected. When it comes, it rarely comes easily. You may still want to talk to them.

Anger. Placing the blame on someone or something—or being mad at the world in general—is how we work to make sense of this new reality.

Bargaining. A sense of inspiration to change the way you negotiate your journey through life. You may have some guilt about what you should have done or said before your parent's passing and promise that you will do things differently in the future.

DEATH OF A PARENT *continues*

Depression. The symptoms associated with depression include a lack of appetite, sleeping too much, and a lack of motivation or energy. Managing these symptoms is key to moving along to the next stage of grief.

Acceptance. The final stage is not about being okay with what happened, but more about acknowledging that this person is really gone and that life in the future will be different.

Begin by writing at least once each day, with a goal of writing every day for the first 30 days. Writing your way through your loss will help you put words to your emotions and your thoughts about your loved one, and can help you process what you are going through. As you cope with the loss and work your way through the grieving process, you may choose to write less often.

Although some days you may not feel like writing anything, journaling is an excellent way to work your way through your grief and gives you a place to put your feelings so that you can get on with your day or get to sleep at night.

For example, it's okay to write just one word, such as "angry," or a short sentence, such as "All I want to do is cry." The goal is to get your feelings out of your head and heart and onto paper. Journaling won't make grief any easier, but it will make it easier to cope with what you're going through.

Job Loss

When it comes to our employment, we like to feel in control. If you've been fired or laid off, it can truly affect your perception of yourself. Many people attach their identity, plus their feelings of competence and self-worth, to their career. Losing your job threatens those feelings. During this time it's important to remember that you were qualified to get this job and you're qualified to get another.

 ## Exercise: Reflecting

Reframe the way you think about this experience, from a loss to an opportunity. This initial step is key to getting your confidence back for the job search that lies ahead. This exercise focuses on acknowledging negative thoughts about yourself and changing them into something positive. Whenever you find yourself thinking that you won't get a job, it will be time for your reframing.

1. Think about what you would like your next job to be and why. Perhaps you have always wanted to do something different and now is the perfect time to rethink your career.
2. Think about your dream employer(s) and plan how you'll make the case for you to get hired, even if it's a position you haven't had before.
3. Does the new job or career require some new education or training?
4. How can you rework your résumé to become the ideal candidate for that dream position?
5. What lessons did you learn from your previous employer and job experience, and how can you apply what you learned with your next employer?

To keep yourself positive and confident, keep thinking about what you do well and what makes you a good employee. Whenever you find yourself doubting your abilities or potential, go back to these thoughts.

Natural Disaster

Life and Mother Nature are far from predictable. If you've been fortunate enough to come through a natural disaster such as a hurricane or earthquake, unscathed, you may know others who haven't been so lucky. Regardless of your outcome, living through a natural disaster can result in depression, anxiety, or even PTSD, depending on your experience. Finding ways to cope as you clean up or try to get back to a normal life is a healthy approach.

 ## Exercise: Movement

This exercise focuses on connecting you with the calmer side of nature. To ensure safety during your practice of the following pose ("asana" in yoga language), steady, even breathing is required, and you should not feel pain.

If you are already something of a yogi, then take your practice outside and perform a series of poses for 15 minutes. Dress as required by the weather and bring a yoga mat if needed. If it is too cold outside, then connect with the outdoors by doing this in front of an open window.

If this is your first exposure to yoga, you will start with a basic standing pose that will introduce you to the practice's calming, centering, and grounding benefits.

The pose you will learn is Mountain Pose (*tadasana*), which is the foundation for all standing poses and is a great "resting" pose. It helps improve balance and posture and foster a calm state.

1. Wear comfortable clothes. If the weather permits, being barefoot is preferable.
2. Stand with your big toes touching and your heels a little apart. If this makes you feel like you are off-balance, stand with your feet hip width apart and parallel, with your toes pointing forward.
3. Spread your toes wide apart and push all four corners of your feet firmly into the ground.
4. Pull your lower ribs inward and press your shoulder blades toward your back, while pushing them down away from your ears.
5. Let your arms hang loosely by your sides with your palms facing forward. Relax your face and make your chin parallel to the floor.
6. Stand straight and tall and align your body as if there is a string running from the center of your pelvis through your spine and through the top of your head.
7. Take five slow and deep breaths while counting from one to three, breathing in through the nose and out through the mouth. Repeat.

Serious Illness

Our health is so precious, but it's also something that we often take for granted—until we find ourselves facing a serious illness. An event such as a heart attack, cancer diagnosis, or other life-threatening illness puts us face-to-face with our mortality. Once in recovery, you may also need to reckon with a new reality. Your new daily routine may require changes not just as you heal but also for longer-term health. Research has shown that positive thoughts can improve the chances of recovery, so focusing on the positive can fuel more optimistic feelings about your future.

 ## Exercise: Reflecting

Because a serious illness changes how we think about ourselves, a reflecting exercise is helpful to challenge the fear, anxiety, sadness, and feelings of loss that may accompany the illness. I suggest that you conduct steps 1 and 2 before you take medica-tion or undergo any treatment for your illness.

1. Begin by thinking about yourself as a warrior fighting your illness.
2. Close your eyes, imagine each cell in your body as a boxer and your illness to be a punching bag, and then think about your cells punching this illness.
3. Once that image is in your mind, take your medication or begin your treatment.
4. If your treatment is something that involves more than taking a pill, then keep this boxing image in your head for as long as your treatment lasts.

This next exercise is to be done every morning when you wake up.

1. Imagine yourself free of your illness in the future and think about the first thing you will do when you are better.
2. No matter what that activity is, focus on that day and that activity and think about how you will feel.
3. Feel that joy. Feel the freedom. And believe it is possible.

Death of a Child

The loss of a child is particularly devastating because it goes against the rules of nature. I want to acknowledge that nothing in this book will alleviate the pain of this type of loss, but you may be able to relieve some of the stress that goes along with all the tasks involved in the death of a loved one.

 ## Exercise: Writing

Grieving is a process, and it does not necessarily end, but this writing exercise will help you celebrate the life of your child and give you an outlet for your feelings. You will be writing a grief journal, and you should write in this journal whenever you feel the need to do so.

1. The goal is to write daily about your memories as well as your feelings, and for the first 30 days there will be no time limit and no page limit.
2. You can write as much or as little as you want, but you should consider writing every day, because connecting with and expressing your deeply felt emotions will help you process them.

After the first month you can begin to incorporate more structure into your writing. However, grief is personal, and your process is yours and yours alone, so if you need to keep your journal unstructured, feel free. When you are ready to have more guidance about what and when to write, then consider the following:

1. In this phase, continue to write every day, but each day pick one memory of your child and focus on one feeling from that memory.
2. You can write as much as you want, but write for no more than half an hour.
3. You can choose to write during whatever part of the day fits best for you.
4. When life may have reverted to a normal schedule and your family and friends have gone back to their lives, allow yourself to have a time and place to grieve every day.
5. Life may be moving on, but your grief won't go away so easily. Honoring your feelings may help you get through the rest of your day.
6. Continue this process for as long as you feel it is necessary.

Chapter 6

Coexisting with Past or Present Trauma

Each person responds to trauma in his or her own unique ways. Many people go on with their lives, but some have a hard time moving on. Trauma can cause physical, psychological, emotional, or spiritual harm. Short-term responses include shock and denial. In the long term, trauma can cause emotional distress, flashbacks, and problems in relationships. Physical symptoms such as insomnia, changes in appetite, headaches, or nausea are common. Another reaction to trauma is post-traumatic stress disorder (PTSD), an anxiety disorder that impacts stress hormones and how the body responds to stress physically, emotionally, and psychologically. PTSD can also cause intense reactions to the memory of the event and can last for years after a traumatic experience.

Abuse or Assault as a Child

In an ideal world, children would always be loved and cared for by the adults in their lives. However, sometimes children are mistreated. Being exposed to emotional, psychological, or physical violence by the people who should protect them—when they are most vulnerable—is the worst kind of violation of trust. This can result in lifelong psychological and emotional effects.

 Exercise: Reflecting

It's important to rethink how you see these events in the larger context of your life. It may take you some time to shift your thinking so that this becomes your default response. It is also important to remember that you cannot change the past and thinking about the what-ifs makes it hard to move beyond what happened. What you can change is the future and how you think about what happened to you in the past. This exercise will focus on shifting your thinking about your role in what happened to you.

1. First, remember that as a child, it was not your responsibility to keep yourself safe. It was the responsibility of the adults and others around you to protect you and take care of you.
2. This was about someone taking advantage of their power or influence to violate someone who was more vulnerable than they were. It was not about you or anything about you.
3. No matter what you did or who you were, you did not deserve to be hurt as a child.
4. To help you remember this, whenever you have memories about what happened to you, tell yourself, "It was not my fault. I did not deserve this."
5. It is also important to tell yourself, "I cannot change what happened to me then, but I can choose how I respond now." This will help give you more of a feeling of control now and in the future, and help counteract the lack of control you felt as a child.

Bullied as a Child

Bullying is unwanted and aggressive behavior—verbal, social, or physical—that uses a power imbalance to control or harm someone else. The behavior is repeated over time and can include physical or verbal attacks, name-calling, humiliation, spreading rumors, making threats, or intentionally excluding someone from a group. Being bullied as a child can be very traumatic and can leave its mark for a lifetime.

 ## Exercise: Writing

Writing about a traumatic event can help you process what happened and help leave it in the past. Perhaps you wrote about your bullying when you were a child, but not being able to do anything about it then must have been very frustrating. As an adult, looking back gives you the gift of perspective.

This exercise will focus on processing the feelings that you still have about the bullying you experienced and help you take back the power that you did not have when you were being bullied.

1. Start by writing about one incident of bullying that you remember.
2. When writing about the story of what happened, you will answer the following questions:

   - Who bullied you?
   - When and where did it happen?
   - Who witnessed the incident?
   - Whom did you report it to?
   - What did they do?
   - If you did not report it to anyone, you should write down why.

3. After you have written the story of one incident, you will write about the feelings that you felt then.

   - Were you angry?
   - Did you feel frustrated?
   - Did you cry?
   - Was there anything you did that made you feel better in the moment?

BULLIED AS A CHILD *continues*

4. Write down what you wish you could have done or said back then to the person(s) who was bullying you.
5. Write about how you feel about the incident now.

   o Do you still feel the same feelings?
   o Are there any lessons that you took from the incident that influence your life now?

6. Next you will answer the following question:

   o What would you say to the person who bullied you if you saw them now?

7. Write what you want to say to them in the form of a letter.
8. At the end of this letter, you will write the following sentence: "What you did to me will no longer control my present or my future."
9. After you are done writing this letter, read it into a mirror as if you are reading it to the person you addressed it to.

10. Now take all the pages you have written and rip them up. Ripping them up is a symbolic gesture of letting go of this memory and the impact it has on you.
11. If you have a wood-burning fireplace, then throw the shredded paper into it and watch it burn. If you don't, then throw it into the garbage or recycling bin.

When you are done with this process, you should feel a sense of relief and perhaps a sense of closure at letting go of a painful memory.

Car Accident

Regardless of whose fault it is and whether or not anyone was injured, being involved in a car accident can be traumatic. The event can cause anxiety about the next time you get into a car, whether or not you are the one in the driver's seat.

 Exercise: Mindfulness

To counteract the anxiety you may feel every time you think about the accident—or even think about getting back into a car or any motorized vehicle—attempt the following exercise in mindfulness to calm those feelings.

More than likely, you have been in many cars over your lifetime, and you have good memories associated with a road trip or with a particular car. For this exercise you will focus on those good memories. The goal is to put the memory of this one traumatic incident into its proper context.

1. Find a quiet, comfortable place to sit.
2. Set a timer to alert you when 10 minutes are up.

3. Close your eyes and think about your fondest road trip memory.
4. Start by thinking about the excitement you felt in planning for the trip.
5. Then focus on the trip itself.

   - Where did you go?
   - Whom did you go with?
   - What stops did you make along the way?
   - What was your favorite moment of the trip?

6. Focus on the favorite moment that you recalled for as long as you can before the 10 minutes are up.
7. In the future, whenever you feel any anxiety related to the car accident, recall this favorite road trip moment.
8. When the feelings arise, close your eyes, and while taking slow, deep breaths in and out, focus on your favorite road trip moment for a count of five, and then open your eyes.

By completing these exercises in mindfulness, your feelings of anxiety will be replaced with feelings of calm and pleasure, and eventually the trauma of the car accident should fade away.

Abuse or Assault as an Adult

Any personal violation that we experience in life can have lasting effects on our feelings of control and safety. One incident can leave its footprint on your psyche; ongoing exposure to abuse can be even more destructive to your emotional and psychological well-being, in addition to any physical injury you may have experienced. You may feel powerless and vulnerable, as well as angry.

 ## Exercise: Movement

The goal of this exercise is to give you back a sense of power and control, and make you feel stronger and perhaps safer. This will be a two-part exercise. The first part will be to do some push-ups to build upper-body strength. The second part will be a boxing exercise, to work on your coordination and confidence. The combined activity will be focused on making you feel stronger and giving you back a feeling of confidence.

1. Begin by putting on comfortable clothes that allow you to move with ease.
2. Assume a proper push-up position.

3. Proceed to do a set of push-ups (1 to 10 push-ups per set).
4. For the first three days you will do however many you can do, and then you will add one more every three days until you get to 10.
5. If you already do push-ups as part of your workout routine, then the goal will be to add another set to your routine.
6. No matter the amount that you decide upon, do not exceed three sets.
7. Repeat these daily exercises for a month.

After you do your push-ups you will move on to part 2 of this exercise. Many people find boxing gives them feelings of power and confidence. It also may help you build some boxing skills! If possible, find a local gym that offers boxing lessons and sign up for one month. Attend class two or three times a week for that month. If you cannot afford the time or money to take a boxing class, then you can do some shadowboxing in the mirror at home and imagine you are punching the person who violated you:

ABUSE OR ASSAULT AS AN ADULT *continues*

1. Begin by facing a mirror.
2. Stand tall with your feet shoulder width apart and your arms hanging relaxed by your sides.
3. Make fists with both hands.
4. Start to punch the air with your dominant hand (if you are right-handed, then use your right hand, and if you are left-handed, then use your left hand).
5. Do the same with your other hand. You will alternately throw 10 punches with each hand.
6. As your strength and skill grow, feel free to add multiple sets of this exercise.
7. Repeat this exercise two to three times a week for a month.

It should be noted that there is no presumption that being physically strong would have prevented what happened to you. This is not about the past, it is about helping you feel stronger and more powerful in the present.

Extramarital Affair

Fidelity is an essential part of the marriage vows and a key expectation of both partners. When someone breaks that vow, it can change the way you perceive your relationship and threaten the hopes you have for your future together. When there is a violation of trust, we often wonder what we did or did not do to make it happen. You may also wonder how you did not know that this was happening.

 ## Exercise: Reflecting

Infidelity can make you feel like you are not enough for your partner. The first part of this reflective exercise is to focus on not blaming yourself for what happened.

1. No matter how difficult your relationship has been, infidelity was a choice that your partner made, and there were lots of other choices that could have been made.
2. Taking responsibility for working on the future of the relationship does not mean that you have to take responsibility for your partner's infidelity.

3. Anytime you find yourself feeling that you are to blame, say to yourself three times: "The affair was not my fault."

The second part of this exercise is to remind yourself that you are enough.

1. Whenever you find yourself thinking that this wouldn't have happened if you had a better body or a prettier face, or were more fun, it is important to remind yourself that nothing about you is responsible for this behavior.
2. Anytime you feel like it is something you are missing that caused your partner to cheat, remind yourself of your worth by repeating three times: "I am enough. I am worthy of the truth. I am worthy of fidelity."

Seriously Ill Parent or Sibling While Growing Up

If your parent or sibling had a serious illness while you were growing up, you may feel as if you did not have the childhood that other children had. You may have had more responsibility as a child than other kids did, or your parent could not do some of the things that you wished they could have done. You may even feel you were cheated out childhood.

 ## Exercise: Writing

This writing exercise will focus on helping you process the thoughts and emotions you have that are related to your childhood experiences growing up in a household that included serious illness in your immediate family.

1. If illness was not always a part of your childhood, begin this exercise by writing one page about what your childhood was like before illness became part of your daily experience.

   o Before your family member became ill, what did they do that you really enjoyed?
   o Write about one of your favorite memories from before their illness.

2. Write a page about when you first found out your parent or sibling was ill and what your reaction was to finding out.

   o How were you told?
   o Who told you?
   o Where were you when you were told?

SERIOUSLY ILL PARENT OR SIBLING
WHILE GROWING UP *continues*

3. The next page you write will be about what changed after illness became a part of your family's life.

   ○ How did your parent/sibling change?
   ○ How did your relationship with your parent/sibling change?
   ○ Did you have to visit them at hospitals?
   ○ How did your role in your family change?
   ○ Did you have to take on more responsibility in the home?
   ○ Did you feel angry or sad that your parent/sibling was ill?
   ○ Did you feel as if life was unfair?

4. On the last page you will write about any life lessons you learned because of your experience. How has the experience made you the person that you are? This section will help you shift your focus from what you lost in your childhood to what you gained in your adulthood.

   ○ How do you think the experience made you a better child/sibling?
   ○ How do you think the experience made you stronger or more grateful?
   ○ How did this experience help you in the life that you live now?

Military Combat

By its very definition, war is traumatizing. Military combat demands that soldiers perform under the most stressful of circumstances. No matter how well trained you are, the challenge of living with the risk of death, or of causing the death of others, can leave an indelible mark on the psyche.

 ## Exercise: Mindfulness

This exercise is not intended to treat PTSD but to help reduce the stress associated with combat experience. Mindfulness can put distance between you and the memories of combat, and give you more of a feeling of control over those memories. Mindfulness can help you focus on the important relationships in your life and on the activities that bring you joy in the present.

Use this exercise to practice awareness and bring your focus to the present. You will deal with the past by focusing on the now. This exercise can be done anywhere, and you should try to make it a routine part of your day.

1. Set aside 5 minutes three times a day to do this exercise. Schedule some time at the beginning, middle, and end of the day. In addition, you can use this exercise any

other time of the day when you need to re-center yourself.

2. Begin by closing your eyes. Focus on your breath as you take in a long, slow, deep inhalation. Feel the air come in through your nose and feel it fill your lungs as your diaphragm expands. Then feel how your body relaxes as the air leaves it.

3. Take a minute to focus on what scents you are smelling in the moment.

   ○ Do you smell food or drink?
   ○ Is there a room fragrance or someone's perfume?

4. With your eyes remaining closed, and while continuing to take deep and slow breaths, take a minute to focus on what you are hearing. Listen to all the sounds around you.

   ○ Whose voices do you hear?
   ○ What noises are in the background?

5. Slowly open your eyes and look around you for 1 minute.

   ○ Is there anything or anyone you notice that you did not notice before?

6. Finish with one slow, deep breath before going back to the rest of your day.

Conclusion

According to the 2015 *Stress in America* survey, women experience more stress than men, and millennials and Gen Xers experience more stress than baby boomers. If you experience sexism, homophobia, or racism, you likely experience more stress than others who are not part of a marginalized group. We can reduce the amount of stress in our lives, but we can't eliminate it; learning how to reduce and manage stress is the best we can do.

A Healthy Response to Stress

As one of the pioneers of stress research, Hans Selye, once noted, "It's not stress that kills us, it's our reaction to it." Stress is not inherently good or bad. How you cope with stress, though, has a direct relation to the various physical, emotional, and psychological impacts that you experience.

It is not realistic or possible to eliminate stress from your life, and so the goal is to control your response to stressful situations. Your body's response includes various functional systems, including your gastrointestinal, respiratory, nervous, endocrine, cardiovascular, and reproductive systems.

Even so, everyone has their own individual set of stress responses. Learning to identify what triggers your stress responses and becoming aware of your unique reactions can help you stay calm and focused in the face of daily stressors. Boosting your emotional resilience can also help you bounce back after being thrown off-balance by a significant unexpected event.

The anxiety you feel before giving a speech is called acute stress. It increases your alertness, and if you are able to channel that feeling in a smart way, it can help you perform at your best. If you don't respond well to stress it can become counterproductive, causing sweaty palms, stomach pain, nausea, or dizziness, and you may not perform as well as you had hoped. When acute stress passes, your body will return to a state of calm.

Living with ongoing chronic stress isn't a healthy way to exist. Your body wasn't meant to stay in a persistent state of heightened arousal. As stated in chapter 1, the flooding of stress hormones— adrenaline and cortisol—into your body for long periods of time can result in an increased risk of hypertension, obesity, diabetes, and cardiovascular disease. Chronic stress may make you feel overwhelmed, and you may find yourself feeling irritable, short-tempered, or more prone to cry. Other symptoms include headaches, stomach problems, and muscle tension in your shoulders, neck, or jaw.

Psychological impacts of exposure to long-term stress can also include anxiety and depression.

No matter the source of your stress, such as finances, relationships, work, or a traumatic experience, a healthy response to stress is possible and is the goal of this book. The harmful effects of stress are determined by the intensity and duration of an experience, but you can respond to challenging and demanding situations by learning how to reframe what you're experiencing. Starting here can help control your physical and psychological response through integrated stress management strategies.

Stress Management Strategies

There are lots of healthy ways to respond to stress. The scenarios for preventing and managing stress described in the various sections of this book are not exhaustive. The hope is that whatever you're experiencing, you should be able to use this book as a resource for finding a similar situation. Although each circumstance comes with a prescriptive exercise, you may find that you prefer one type of response over another. Movement may end up as your preferred way of dealing with stress, or perhaps writing is best at helping you sort through your emotions. Just know that there is no one way of dealing with a stressful situation.

My hope is that all readers can find something that works for them based on their own unique stress response and preferred activities. Some of the exercises that I have outlined can be incorporated into a daily routine of stress management; these include mindfulness practices, journaling of emotions, and physical activity such as yoga. A daily routine of stress management strategies builds emotional resilience and reduces vulnerability to stress.

Going Forward

We face stressful situations all the time: a difficult exam, being stuck in traffic, problems in relationships with people we love. The unpredictability of life means that at one time or another we will all be faced with a challenging event, such as a death or illness, that throws us off-balance and has us feeling overwhelmed. This is why building emotional resilience is so important. It is not enough to wait until bad things happen to deal with them, because we can prepare emotionally for the challenges of life before they come our way.

It's important to find stress management strategies and incorporate them into your everyday life. Starting the day with some mindfulness is a great way to get you centered, balanced, and calm. Medical experts say that "sitting is the new smoking" because our increasingly sedentary lifestyle is no good for our health. With this in mind, movement is another great way to start the day. It can wake you up and get your blood flowing. It's also unhealthy for our mental health and brain function to sit in front of our devices. Breaking up the workday with some movement is a great prescription. Journaling is another excellent way to relieve stress, especially if you include gratitude. Writing helps you process feelings and thoughts; putting them all on paper takes them off your mind. At the end of the day, stress management techniques can be integrated into your evening routine so that you can shed the stress of the day, relax, and sleep well.

It is possible for you to have a healthy response to stress. Developing an awareness of what triggers your stress response can help you see it coming and prepare for it. And even if you don't see it coming, when you develop stress management strategies that work to keep you mentally and physically healthy and happy, you can achieve anything, no matter what life throws at you.

Resources

Books

Carlson, Richard. *Don't Sweat the Small Stuff . . . and It's All Small Stuff: Simple Ways to Keep the Little Things from Taking Over Your Life.* New York: Hachette Books, 1997.

Farrarons, Emma. *The Mindfulness Coloring Book.* New York: Boxtree, 2015.

Greenberg, Melanie. *The Stress-Proof Brain: Master Your Emotional Response to Stress Using Mindfulness and Neuroplasticity.* Oakland, CA: New Harbinger, 2017.

Hanson, Rick, and Forrest Hanson. *Resilient: How to Grow an Unshakable Core of Calm, Strength, and Happiness.* San Jose: Harmony, 2018.

Kabat-Zinn, Jon. *Full Catastrophe Living: Using the Wisdom of Your Body and Mind to Face Stress, Pain, and Illness* (revised). New York: Bantam, 2013.

McGonigal, Kelly. *The Upside of Stress: Why Stress Is Good for You, and How to Get Good at It.* New York: Avery, 2015.

Sapolsky, Robert M. *Why Zebras Don't Get Ulcers.* 3rd ed. New York: Holt, 2004.

Seligman, Martin. *Authentic Happiness: Using the New Positive Psychology to Realize Your Potential for Lasting Fulfillment.* New York: Free Press, 2002.

Selye, Hans. *The Stress of Life.* New York: McGraw-Hill, 1978.

Shrand, Joseph, and Leigh Devine. *Manage Your Stress: Overcoming Stress in the Modern World.* New York: St. Martin's Griffin, 2012.

Sockolov, Matthew. *Practicing Mindfulness: 75 Essential Meditations to Reduce Stress, Improve Mental Health, and Find Peace in the Everyday.* Oakland, CA: Althea Press, 2018.

Sood, Amit, and Mayo Clinic. *The Mayo Clinic Handbook for Happiness: A 4-Step Plan for Resilient Living.* New York: De Capo Lifelong Books, 2015.

Thich Nhat Hanh. *The Miracle of Mindfulness: An Introduction to the Practice of Meditation.* Boston: Beacon, 1999.

Reports

Goh, Joel, Jeffrey Pfeffer, and Stefanos A. Zenios. *Workplace Stressors & Health Outcomes: Health Policy for the Workplace.* Behavioral Science & Policy Association, February 17, 2017. behavioralpolicy.org/articles/workplace-stressors -health-outcomes-health-policy-for-the-workplace.

Stress in America. American Psychological Association, 2019. www.apa.org/news/press/ releases/stress/2019/stress-america-2019.pdf.

Stress in America: Paying with Our Health. American Psychological Association, 2015. apa.org/news /press/releases/stress/2014/stress-report.pdf.

Stress Management: Enhance Your Well-Being by Reducing Stress and Building Resilience. Harvard Medical School Special Health Report, 2016.

Organizations

The American Institute of Stress

www.stress.org
Diverse and inclusive, the American Institute of Stress educates medical practitioners, scientists, health care professionals, and the public; conducts research; and provides information, training, and techniques to prevent human illness related to stress.

American Psychological Association

apa.org/topics/stress
American Psychological Association, Center for Organizational Excellence, Resources for Employers

APA is the leading scientific and professional organization representing psychology in the United States, with more than 121,000 researchers, educators, clinicians, consultants, and students as its members.

Global Organization for Stress

gostress.com
The Global Organization for Stress is an independent global association dedicated to dealing with stress-related issues around the world.

The Stress Institute

stressinstitute.com
The Stress Institute is a center for the collection and dissemination of information on the impact of stress on health and provides stress reduction and mindfulness training.

The Stress Management Society

stress.org.uk
The Stress Management Society is a nonprofit organization dedicated to helping individuals and companies recognize and reduce stress.

Stress Research Institute, Stockholm University

stressforskning.su.se/english/research
The Stress Research Institute is a national knowledge center focusing on stress reactions, sleep, and health. The institute is part of the Faculty of Social Sciences at Stockholm University.

Stress Management Tips

100 Motivational Quotes That Will Relieve Your Stress

inc.com/lolly-daskal/100-motivational-quotes
-that-will-relieve-your-stress.html

American Heart Association

heart.org/HEARTORG/HealthyLiving
/StressManagement/Stress-Management
_UCM_001082_SubHomePage.jsp

Be Well at Work, UC Berkeley

uhs.berkeley.edu/sites/default/files
/wellness-healthyoffice-stress.pdf

National Alliance on Mental Illness

nami.org/Find-Support/Living-with-a-Mental
-Health-Condition/Managing-Stress

Stress Tip Sheet, American Psychological Association

apa.org/news/press/releases/2007/10
/stress-tips.aspx

Stress Assessment Tests

HealthyPlace
healthyplace.com/psychological-tests
/online-stress-test

Holmes & Rahe Stress Test
mindtools.com/pages/article/newTCS_82.htm

Mental Health America
mentalhealthamerica.net/stress-screener

**Perceived Stress Scale by Sheldon Cohen
(hosted by Mind Garden)**
mindgarden.com/documents
/PerceivedStressScale.pdf

Psychologist World
psychologistworld.com/stress/stress-test

Psychometrics
psychometrics.com/assessments/stress-profile

Stress Management Society
stress.org.uk/individual-stress-test

Support Groups

Beyond My Battle
beyondmybattle.org

Reduces the stress of serious illness, rare disease, and disability through emotional support and educational resources rooted in mindfulness, awareness, and compassion.

Psychology Today
psychologytoday.com/us/groups/stress

Psychology Today is a magazine and comprehensive resource directory of therapists, psychiatrists, treatment facilities, and mental health resources.

Index

Acknowledgments

I want to thank Carolyn Abate—my editor at Callisto Media—for her patience and support. Thanks to my daughter, Maya, for always inspiring me to "just do it." I am grateful for the patience of my USC students as I juggled a new heavy teaching schedule while writing this book. Writing books was never something I planned to do and would not have done were it not for the strong encouragement of my father, who thought this was what I should do, even though I thought I had nothing to say, which is not something anyone else would say about me. I will forever be indebted to Pam Lipp—a mentor who helped me find my purpose in reducing the stress and building the resilience of workforces everywhere. Thank you to Chris Wilcox for his friendship and support and for pushing me to expand the vision I had for myself. Thanks also go to all the people with whom I have had the privilege of sharing my knowledge of stress management and beating burnout and compassion fatigue; your questions, comments, and engagement have made our sessions fun and built my knowledge and expertise.

About the Author

Ruth C. White, PhD, is on a mission to create and support healthier and happier workplaces, workforces, and communities. Dr. White is a clinical associate professor in the Suzanne Dworak-Peck School of Social Work at the University of Southern California, where she teaches leadership, management, and social policy to graduate students.

Inspired by her own journey of illness, recovery, and resilience with bipolar disorder, she is a mental health advocate and activist who promotes mental health and well-being by speaking and writing on stress management, mental wellness, and the stigma of mental illness, with an approach that is holistic, science based, and prevention focused.

With more than 20 years of public speaking experience, Dr. White has built a reputation for thought-provoking keynotes, lectures, presentations, and workshops that lead to paradigm shifts, organizational change, and personal growth. Through her collaborative partners, she has helped build, implement, manage, and evaluate programs in health, mental health, social welfare, and diversity inclusion.

Dr. White was born in London and grew up in Jamaica and Canada. When she is not indulging her wanderlust, she can be found in her home base of Oakland, California, walking Lake Merritt. Passionate about being outside, she is an avid hiker, sailor, and kayaker. Her favorite travel and adventure partner is her only child, Maya.

For more information, you can find her on LinkedIn or check out her website at ruthcwhite.com.

CPSIA information can be obtained
at www.ICGtesting.com
Printed in the USA
JSHW012242230420
5238JS00008BA/23

9 781646 115761